# British Railways In And Around The Midlands

# 1953-57

by
John Cowlishaw

BOOK LAW PUBLICATIONS

2

*First published in the United Kingdom by Book Law Publications*
*382 Carlton Hill, Nottingham, NG4 1JA*
*Printed & bound by The Amadeus Press, Cleckheaton, West Yorkshire*

# Foreword

My interest in railways stemmed from my father, who worked for the London, Midland & Scottish Railway and then British Railways. As a result until I was sixteen I was able to travel extensively on free passes or P.T.'s (Privilege Ticket at a quarter fare). I started taking photographs in earnest during 1954 (aged fifteen), all of those in this album being taken with a Zeiss Nettar (2 ¼ squared) with a top speed of 1/250 second which somewhat limited the scope a little. The camera must have been a gift, as I could only afford to have selected shots printed. The rest stayed in a Coronation biscuit tin, never printed, until 2004 when I bought a scanner to see what they looked like. Fortunately, I had kept all of my notes covering numbers, locations and dates.

Based in Nottingham, I toured around by train and bicycle, but also on shed tours organised by the local branch of the Railway Correspondence & Travel Society and a model railway shop in Nottingham run by a Mr Gibbon, a remarkable man who was totally deaf and unable to speak. Tours of Derby works were available and I would also spend days on New Street station in Birmingham (and Snow Hill, the nearest I could get to the Great Western). I went on a tour of the Leicester West Bridge line on a WEA course with C.R.Clinker, a noted historian of the time. Crewe was also a magnet, although I never went round the locomotive works or engine sheds for some reason. We always travelled LMS where possible, to London always via Melton Mowbray, where I had relatives, never via Leicester, and certainly never by the Great Central route.

One of the highlights, amongst many, was a tour by a then new diesel multiple unit set, from Nottingham to Betwys-y-Coed, passing as it did through Derby, Stoke, Crewe, Chester and North Wales, a spotter's paradise, all for a cost of, I think, 7/6d.

My interest waned in 1959 when I joined the Territorial Army, and then got married. Our honeymoon hotel was near Bournemouth (Central) station, which I regretfully, in 1963, never visited. I resumed interest, with colour slides and prints, in the 1970's, in both BR and preserved railways. I now spend time a the Great Central Railway in Loughborough, somewhere I never gave a thought to in the fifties.

The photographs used in this album cover a geographical area based around the Midlands of England. That is the North Midlands, East Midlands, South Midlands and the West Midlands. Where one draws a boundary in this diverse landscape, to qualify a location by title, I am not certain but perhaps you will forgive me if I have put your local station in the wrong 'Midlands'.

I have not covered every nook and cranny at any one location (if only I could have done - with hindsight). Furthermore, I have arranged the selection of venues in an anti-clockwise direction although some deviation was necessary to cover such a broad canvas. Hopefully, you will find my nostalgic journey as appealing and satisfying as I did.

*John Cowlishaw, Bardney, 2005.*

Horwich built Stanier Cl.5 No.44685, then barely five years old, passes beneath the signal gantry at the north end of Chester (General) station after turning on the nearby triangle on Saturday 28th May 1955. This engine was one of only ten of the class fitted with SKF roller bearings on all axles. No.44685 did not have a long life compared with others in the class, the BR policy of banishing steam in 1968 put paid to any longevity planned prior to its building. However, after leaving Horwich works for Crewe North in July 1950, the engine settled down to a fairly long relationship with the shed and except for an eight week loan to Northampton over the Christmas and New Year period of 1951-52, it was at 5A until closure of the shed in May 1965 when it moved across town to the South shed. Withdrawal came in April 1967 at a time when any steam locomotive failure, no matter how minor, usually meant condemnation and the scrapyard. On the right of this picture is the former Great Western engine shed with a couple of Swindon's products simmering in the afternoon sun. The depot consisted two building in BR days, the nearest one dated from 1856 and was opened by the Chester & Birkenhead Railway. In 1928 the GWR fitted a new roof and improved some of the existing facilities. The other shed, just visible in the background, was even older being built by the Chester & Crewe Railway in 1840. When the LNWR vacated the place in 1870 for new larger premises it had built to the east of the station, the old shed was handed over to the GWR. Going full circle, the 1840's shed became the property of the LM Region after the formation of BR and the shed was reroofed in 1957. Closed to steam in 1960, it then became a diesel depot.

After working into Chester (General) from Rhyl with a stopping train on 28th May 1955, BR Standard No.78034 now waits to turn on the triangle ready for its return working. New to Rhyl 6K shed in October 1954, this 2-6-0 was one of five new Class 2s allocated to the North Wales depot in the autumn of 1954. Their arrival saw the last of Rhyl's resident 2P 4-4-0s banished to the scrapheap but the new engines were transferred to the less salubrious surroundings of Widnes in May 1956 and their place taken by five of the Ivatt LMS version of this same design. During their short time in North Wales the class was normally used on the stopping services to Chester, Bangor and Denbigh and, during the holiday season of 1955, on the *North Wales Land Cruise* trains which worked out to Portmadoc from Rhyl via Corwen and then back along the coast line through Bangor. During its short lifetime this particular Cl.2 was also allocated to Bangor, Watford, Willesden and finally Crewe South from where it was withdrawn in January 1966. Not one of the lucky ones, 78034 was purchased by T.W.Ward and cut up in their Killamarsh scrapyard in he summer of 1966. In the left background, under the road bridge, can be seen Collett 2-8-0 No.2890 stabled on the former Great Western shed at Chester West, 84K.

A fine study of 'Royal Scot' No.46167 THE HERTFORDSHIRE REGIMENT standing by a water column at the south end of Chester (General) station. On the right a mineral wagon still wears its private owner markings some fifteen years or more after being taken over by the Government. Saturday, 28th May 1955.

Lamped up and ready now to take its train off to the south, No.46167 of Crewe North awaits its signal on this busy early summer Saturday. During its life thirty-four year life, this Derby built 'Scot' was allocated to ten different depots from Carlisle to London and from Holyhead to Annesley. It had seven separate stints at Crewe North, three at Camden, two each at Holyhead, Longsight, Preston and Upperby, and a single stay at Bushbury, Springs Branch, Willesden and Annesley, its last shed. It was condemned in April 1964.

Entering the station with empty stock, Crewe North 'Jubilee', No.45634 TRINIDAD will drop off its train prior to proceeding to the triangle to 'turn' and face the right way for its homeward journey on Saturday, 28th May 1955.

As the afternoon of Saturday 28th May 1955 wore on at Chester (General), the frequency of trains did not alter as this view of the southern end of the platforms testifies. Stanier Class 5's 45130, 45062 and 44685 all await their turn for the 'off'. Mold Junction Cl.5 No.45130 is waiting to take on a Manchester bound train, Grimesthorpe's No.45062 is ready with its Sheffield bound train whilst 44685 awaits an incoming train. Resident BR Standard Cl.4 No.75039 completes the line-up.

Missing shedplates became a normal occurrence in the 1960's but in May 1955 it was unusual to see a steam locomotive bereft of such identification. BR Standard Cl.4 No.75039 is making do with a crudely painted version of 6A on the 28th May even though it had been transferred to Chester shed three months previously, along with 75033, 75034 and 75035 from Bletchley. Now nearly two years old, the 4-6-0 is looking decidedly grubby as it awaits a signal at Chester (General) station. Chester shed, which generally had a half dozen of these particular Standard 4's at its disposal, used them on semi-fasts to Manchester (Exchange), Liverpool (Lime Street) and westwards to Bangor. Throughout its fourteen year lifetime, this engine was allocated to seven different sheds on the London Midland Region, its longest stay was the seven years spent at Chester before returning to Bletchley in March 1962. Having spent much of 1967 in storage, No.75039 was withdrawn from Tebay shed in September of that year and by February 1968 it was in the hands of the Motherwell Machinery and Scrap Co.

Saturday 28th May 1955. We are at the south end of Crewe station watching the fireman of 9A Longsight based 'Royal Scot' No.46131 THE ROYAL WARWICKSHIRE REGIMENT, top up the tender with water prior to departure for Shrewdbury with a train from Manchester to Swansea. During its thirty-four year career, this 'Scot' had first started its operational life at Polmadie shed, carrying the name PLANET. Its February 1932 move to Crewe North shed signalled that it would never be allocated to a Scottish shed again and was to spend the next twenty-odd years working over the old LMS Western Division. In September 1932 it was allocated to Longsight shed for the first time. Just under three years later it returned to Crewe North for a two month stint prior to moving over to Holyhead. During its two year stay at the Anglesey shed it was renamed and came into the Regimental fold. Leaving Holyhead in February 1938, it went direct to Longsight but stayed there only until November when Crewe North beckoned once again, this time for a six year spell through the Second World War. As the wartime demands on the railways changed during the conflict, LMS locomotive operating policy changed to suit the prevailing conditions and in early 1944, when Crewe North shed had only one 'Duchess' allocated, no less than twenty-six 'Scots' were 'in residence' at the depot. No.6131 was one of nine of the class rebuilt in 1944 with a 2A boiler and double chimney and in January 1945 it moved briefly to Holyhead shed in its new guise before returning to 5A for another two years. Longsight got it back in April 1947 albeit for only six months, then it went onto Camden, its first such allocation to a London depot. By Christmas it was back at Longsight for its longest stay at any shed during its life. In October 1957 No.46131 moved down to London again but this time onto the old Midland Division for a nine month stay at Kentish Town depot after which it went back to Manchester but to Trafford Park shed where for a few weeks it helped out on the Manchester (Central) - St Pancras expresses. Then it returned to London and the Western Lines at Camden shed. A month later it went to Crewe North again but in November it went to Longsight, its fourth move that year. By now the rebuilt 'Scot' was getting worn out, even after general repair and it moved from Longsight after the arrival of the English Electric Type 4 diesels at the Manchester depot. Millhouses was its next shed and from February 1960 until December 1961 it worked the main line expresses to London as well as stopping services to places such as Stockport and Manchester. With the imminent closure of Millhouses shed, the 'Scot' moved across to the north-east side of Sheffield to another former Midland shed at Canklow. With little or no appropriate work available, and in a less than ideal condition, it moved back to the Western Lines in March 1962 being allocated to Llandudno Junction, its last shed before withdrawal which occurred in October 1962. Appropriately Crewe works, where the engine had received all of its repairs, cut up No.46131 later that year.

On the same day, another 'Royal Scot', No.46164 THE ARTISTS RIFLEMAN of Edge Hill shed, waits for the Liverpool portion of a northbound express (probably the *PINES EXPRESS*) which will be split here at Crewe. Rebuilt as late as 1951, No.46164 was not the last of the class to receive the 2A boiler and a double chimney; that honour went to No.46137 during the same year when this photograph was taken. One of the twenty Derby-built 'Scots', 6164 started life in September 1930 at Longsight shed without a name but this was rectified in 1932 upon its move to Carlisle Upperby shed. By the end of that year it was back in Manchester with fellow 'Scots' 6165 to 6169. In July 1936 Bangor shed employed it for four months prior to a move to Crewe North. It spent much of the war years at Edge Hill and only left there in September 1959 when the big diesels started to arrive. 5A was once again home for this 4-6-0 but not for long and in February 1960 it followed No.46131 to Millhouses depot in Sheffield. By now the pair became seemingly inseparable and went together to Canklow roundhouse for storage and not much else. However, even though 46164 would have enjoyed a final move to North Wales with 46131 in March 1962, it had to make do with the short move to Darnall in June. Withdrawn in December of that year, it finally met up with 46131 again during the great gathering of 1962 at Crewe works when nearly half of the class were scrapped.

Great Western engines had been seen at Crewe since the earliest days and in September 1955 you could still catch a dozen or more working into the town. They even had their own shed at Gresty Lane where, on a good weekend, 'Halls', 'Granges', and all types of Swindon built engines could be viewed. The all stations Crewe to Wellington via Market Drayton service was in the main handled by 0-6-0 Pannier tanks and on Saturday 3rd September 1955, Collett 0-6-0PT No.5719 works back to Wellington bunker first with a late afternoon service. Built over the twenty year period from 1929 to 1949, this version of the inside cylinder, 4ft 7½in. 'Panniers' was confined mainly to short haul goods work and yard shunting. However quite a number were vacuum fitted and were used, like No.5719 on passenger working. Wellington based Ivatt 2-6-2 tank engines had taken over these services by the end of the decade but their reign was short-lived as the line was closed, a victim of the 'Beeching Axe'.

On one of the through lines found on the western boundary of Crewe station, ex GWR Churchward 2-6-0 No.6339 of Croes Newydd shed, has stopped for signals whilst heading a football excursion from Wrexham made up of non-corridor stock running under express headlamps. The photographic vantage point from where this scene was recorded on 3rd September 1955, was the footbridge which linked the station with a 'cindered' path leading to Crewe North engine shed. The mid afternoon sun bathes the subject and its surroundings with equal intensity. Such was the spread of Crewe station, it was possible to miss one or two of the non-stop through workings during busy periods - it was definately a place to have your wits about you.

Local boy No.45684, 'Jubilee' JUTLAND and unrebuilt 'Patriot' No.45533 LORD RATHMORE of Edge Hill shed, await the signal which will give them passage to the shed at Crewe North on 28th May 1955. Both engines have worked in independently on trains from the north but to save line occupation they have been coupled together for the short trip from the south end of the station to the shed. Note the lattice girder footbridge from which a couple of these Crewe photographs were captured on film.

Watching trains on summer Saturdays in the 1950's was a pleasure whichever location you chose. Busy junctions and main line locations out in the country all had their fascinations but rail centres such as Crewe could boast virtually continuous movement throughout the day with old favourites coming and going along with the occasional surprise. It all added up to one thing - pure enjoyment. In this scene at the north end of Crewe station in May 1955, Patricroft 'Jubilee' No.45674 DUNCAN, in a dubious external condition, is getting ready to head off to Manchester or Liverpool with a train from South Wales. A Patricroft engine since March 1939, 45674 transferred to Saltley in March 1963 breaking a twenty-four year link with the Lancashire depot.

*(opposite)* An unusual and revealing view of LORD RATHMORE from the lattice girder footbridge. The crewmen both appear to have white collared shirts, and I should imagine their boots were clean too - such was the pride of the express locomotive footplatemen even during the 1950's. The 3,500 gallon tender has the small BR emblem as opposed to the large emblem applied to the Stanier 4,000 gallon tenders seen on the 'Jubilee' and the 'Royal Scots' illustrated so far. Note the coal is depleted though by no means exhausted indicating that 45533 has worked in from somewhere such as Blackpool or even Llandudno. Besides the dubious quality of the coal, take a look at the position of the fire irons which are tucked well out of the way. With the coming of electrification and the fact that old habits die hard, one can understand the need to warn fireman of the dangers of climbing into tenders for whatever reason. Withdrawn in September 1962, this unrebuilt 'Patriot' was amongst the last of its kind and one of the twenty-four original examples of the class to be scrapped that year.

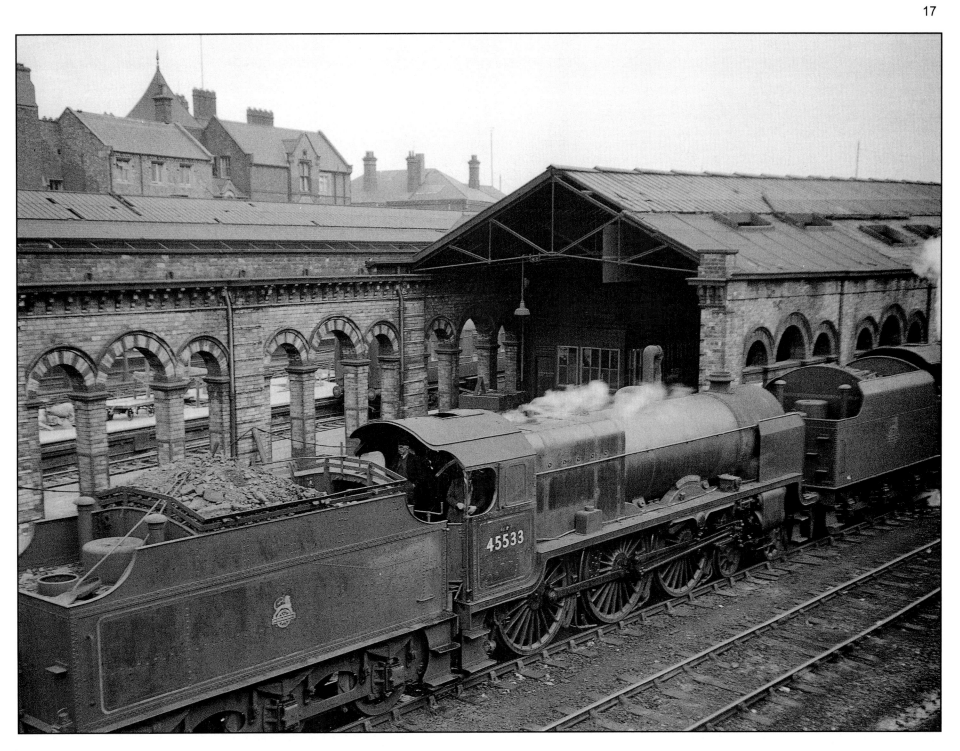

Longsight Class 5 Caprotti No.44748 is turned and ready to work back to Manchester on Wednesday, 22nd August 1956 at Shrewsbury shed. This particular Class 5 was non-standard to the majority of the class and besides the valve gear it was also equipped with Timken roller bearings on every axle. These Class 5 derivatives were, in the main, as successful as the orthodox engines but required perhaps slightly more maintenance time. No doubt if their planned 30-35 year working lifespan had gone the full course they would have shown an improvement in performance and savings in running costs over the majority of the class. But, the twenty-two Caprotti equipped engines were not to get a full working life and most were amongst the early withdrawals of the long-lived Class 5's. Five went in 1963, ten the following year, five in 65, and the last two, Nos.44687 and 44743 in 1966 when more than half of the class were still active. No.44748 spent all of its life at Longsight shed from new in February 1948 to its August 1964 withdrawal. Behind the Caprotti is a visiting WD 2-8-0 (unidentified I'm afraid) which was in a worst external condition than 44748 - weren't all the WD's filthy all of the time except when ex works? Prior to the Normandy landing and the eventual liberation of Europe, Shrewsbury engine shed had ten WD 2-8-0's on loan, along with one of the American built S160 class 2-8-0's. The engines are stabled on what might have been termed the LMS side of the depot prior to nationalisation and the northlight roof on this shed gives away its LNWR origins. Shrewsbury Coleham, to give the place its full name, was truly a joint shed, albeit with a hidden demarcation line. Engine sheds were established on this site as early as 1852 by the Shrewsbury & Hereford Railway and these in turn were taken over by the Great Western who also built a roundhouse in 1883. The LNWR had also utilised another of the S&HR buildings as an engine shed in the early 1860's and in 1877 built the ten road northlight shed partly in view here. The LMS maintained an allocation of about seventy locomotives here whilst the GWR generally housed slightly less than that. Shrewsbury Coleham lasted as a steam locomotive shed until November 1967 and was afterwards used to stable visiting diesel locomotives for a few years.

The north end of Shrewsbury station on the afternoon of Wednesday 22nd August 1956 with a big engine and a small train. Being a weekday this is one of the numerous 'running-in' turns undertaken from Crewe in order to test locomotives ex works after repair. The three non-corridor coaches are hardly a trial for 'Jubilee' No.45624 ST. HELENA, but it is enough of a load to find any problems prior to being sent back to its home shed at Longsight. Like many other new LMS 5XP 4-6-0's, this engine ran for nearly two years before it was named in 1936. During its twenty-nine year operational life it was allocated to eight different sheds with four visits to Camden, two visits each to Crewe North, Longsight and Willesden, and a single stay at Chester, Leeds Holbeck, Nuneaton and Rugby. Withdrawal took place in November 1963 and it was cut up at its birthplace - Crewe works - in March 1964.

The former Midland Railway engine shed at Saltley in Birmingham consisted three roundhouses joined together in the form of a letter 'L'. The first of these sheds dated from 1868 with the second being added I 1876 and the last one as late as 1900. The building suffered the ravages of time, pollution and weather over the years and it fell to BR to reroof all three of the sheds. On a 16th September 1956 visit to the depot, the roof of this particular shed, No.3 I think, was still open to the elements which although bad for the stabled locomotives, was great for my photography. This group of Stanier engines, flanked on the right by BR Standard Cl.5 No.73049, consists left to right Cl.5 No.44848, Cl.8F No.48338, Cl.5 No.44841, and Cl.8F No.48687. The latter three appear to be in excellent external condition and are all Saltley based engines. No.44848 was Derby shedded on this date and had started life on the Midland Division at Holbeck shed in November 1944. Saltley acquired it during the first month of BR's existence but lost it to Derby the following October. In July 1953 it went on a two month loan to Kingmoor but on its return south it was allocated to Millhouses. Derby got it back in October 1955. Leicester was its next shed, in January 1959, and from there it ventured onto the old Great Central main line with a move to Leicester GC shed in March 1962. Annesley was its next port of call in July 1964 and it worked from there until closure of both that shed and the GC main line in January 1966. For convenience it then went to nearby Colwick but only until April when it undertook its last reallocation, moving into the territory which became the last stronghold of BR steam. It worked for nearly two years from Rose Grove but finally gave in during February 1968. Its last journey took it to Cohen's scrapyard at Kettering. 8F No.48338 was a recent arrival at Saltley, coming from Toton in July. It went back to Toton in March 1958 and over the next ten years was allocated to eight different depots, ending up at Patricroft from where it was withdrawn in May 1968. It too went to Cohen's for scrap. No.44841 arrived at Saltley, for the first time, in October 1944 and two years later moved to Nottingham. In October 1951 it returned to Saltley to enjoy a fourteen year residence only broken by a two month loan to Leicester GC shed in 1958. A move to Oxley in April 1965 was its last and it was condemned there in October 1966. Staying 'local', it was purchased by Cashmores and went to their Great Bridge yard in January 1968. Brighton built 8F No.48687 went new to Shrewsbury in February 1944 and going by way of Crewe South, Buxton and Barrow Hill, ended up at Saltley in June 1947. Another long time resident, the 8F left Birmingham for Coalville in November 1960. Following the declining traffic, it went to another three sheds before Newton Heath depot withdrew it shortly after arrival in May 1968. 48687 was scrapped at Drapers in Hull. Standard No.73049 was, in 1956, allocated to Bath Green Park engine shed and even though it was less than three years old, it would have a shorter working life than the ex LMS engines being withdrawn in March 1965. Incidentally, all the Stanier engines were built in 1944, the 5's at Crewe, 48338 at Horwich and 48687 at Brighton.

At one time the former London & North Western depot at Monument Lane consisted two engine sheds dating from different periods. The earliest shed, a three road affair, was erected in 1858 but was demolished in 1932. The second shed, the six road dead-end building seen here, was built in 1884. Throughout most of its life the depot had been home to a stud of engines consisting passenger and goods locomotives, both tender and tank types alike, the latter working many of the local services from New Street station. The shed was never home to the more glamorous 'namers' but visiting engines of that ilk were regularly found on the yard for servicing. Camden based 'Jubilee' No.45686 ST. VINCENT was one such visitor on Sunday 16th September 1956. During its twenty-six year career, this 'Jubilee' had just three homes, albeit on numerous occasions. Crewe North was its first abode and also during a further two periods. Carnforth was its next shed, and its last because it was condemned in November 1962 after a three year stay. Camden depot had it for four months in the late 1930's but got it again in February 1953 for a six year residence. Its maker, Crewe works scrapped it in late 1962.

Most of the express passenger trains travelling over the old LMS route from the West Midlands to London Euston started their journey at Wolverhampton (High Level) station and called at Birmingham (New Street) en route. Therefore, although Aston had its fair share of the larger express motive power used on those and other expresses, Bushbury engine shed housed the bulk of the motive power responsible for those trains. Situated on the north side of Wolverhampton, the former LNWR engine shed at Bushbury had origins dating back to 1859 but the eight road shed used by British Railways became operational in 1883. Both the LMS and BR invested a lot of money into this establishment, the former building a mechanical coaling plant and an ash handling plant whilst BR put a new roof on the shed in the late 1950's. From their introduction the 'Patriot' and 'Jubilee' classes have worked from Bushbury depot over the years and whilst a third of the former class have been allocated at one time or another, some forty-seven different 'Jubilees' have served the place. The 'Royal Scots' did not make any inroads into the allocation until they began to be displaced from other main line work by the growing diesel fleet on the London Midland Region and then no less than eighteen of the class came and went during the early years of 1960's. 'Patriot' No.45539 E.C.TRENCH, standing alongside the ash plant on 16th September 1956, is typical of the express motive power gracing he shed at that period and has just worked in from Euston. Note the 3,500 gallon straight high sided tender (No.4573) which was originally attached to 'Jubilee' No.5616 MALTA when new but 'joined' the Patriot class in December 1942 when it was attached to unnamed No.5550. No.45539 got it 1st May 1956 but gave it up to No.45515 CAERNARVON in January of the following year.

Another depot on the itinerary during the RCTS 'shed bash' by coach in September 1956 was Aston. This place was another ex LNWR engine shed which was still operating having been rebuilt towards the end of the LMS period. Situated some distance from New Street station, compared with Monument Lane, the 1883 built shed was a much larger building consisting of twelve roads with a more spacious yard. Residents during my visit were mainly Stanier designed engines including 2-6-4T No.42470, which had come new from Derby in November 1936. Transferred away to Watford in February 1961, this tank had one more shed to call home - Willesden - before being condemned in September 1962. Since the introduction of the Stanier 2-cylinder 2-6-4T in 1935, no less than twenty-nine of the type were allocated to Aston at one time or another. On the right is Caprotti '5' No.44748 which spent the whole of its short sixteen year life allocated to Longsight shed from February 1948 to August 1964 when it was condemned. Aston engine shed lasted a while longer; closing in October 1965. It was later demolished.

A set of Cheshire Lines Committee articulated coaches in use at Birmingham (New Street) in August 1955. Far from home territory, the set includes a brake composite and was quite a surprise.

New Street station, Saturday 27th August 1955 with Bushbury 'Jubilee' No.45737 ATLAS at the head of a midday London bound express. No.45737 had been allocated to Bushbury shed on four different occasions, the earliest in 1939, prior to this residence which had started in July 1951 and ended in February 1960 when it moved on to Aston for four months before a two year stint at Crewe North. From Crewe it went to its final shed, Newton Heath in April 1962 and enjoyed nearly two years of working from there before being withdrawn. It was cut up at the West of Scotland Shipbreaking yard in Troon, where a number of other distinguished notables among them seven 'Duchesses', were also scrapped. Note the loaded trolley on the platform, a reminder of the days when the railways carried much of the nation's goods and parcels.

At virtually the same spot as the previous photograph, and a little later on the same day, another 'Jubilee' occupies the platform with a London bound working. This engine, No.45740 MUNSTER, was Camden based and had been since June 1953. Built at Crewe in December 1936, its first depot was Crewe North. In March 1939 it moved to Aston for the duration of the war and the following eight years before its transfer to London. It was to return to Aston shortly before withdrawal in October 1963 but before then it had moved to Willesden from Camden, then in September 1960 it went to Llandudno Junction for nine months prior to returning to Crewe North and then retracing its earlier steps to Aston.

BR Standard 9F 2-10-0 No.92079 was given the Lickey banking job in May 1956, shortly after entering traffic at Toton shed. In this Sunday 16th September 1956 front end view the 2-10-0 is resting on the Bromsgrove coal stage line awaiting the next job to come along. The large headlight was the one reputedly carried by the most famous of all the Lickey 'bankers' the Midland Railway 0-10-0 No.58100 which had the nickname 'Big Bertha'. The 9F took over from the large lady and worked the incline until October 1963 when diesel locomotives took on the job. The incline banking job has attracted some of the best and worse, as well as large and small locomotives over the years. The LNER Class U1 Garratt, No.69999, joined the throng here for a couple of stints, one in 1949 as a coal burner and then in the summer of 1955 as an oil burner. Both visits were undistinguished, the authorities wanted to find the right sort of work for the huge locomotive whilst the footplatemen at Bromsgrove did not take kindly to the articulated giant and were, it seems, determined not to make it work.

This frontal three-quarter view of 92079 at Bromsgrove is a nice study of this impressive 9F. After its eight years of employment pushing trains, the 2-10-0 went off to Birkenhead shed and had a further four years pulling them before premature withdrawal in November 1967. An engine shed for housing the locomotives used as banking engines on the Lickey incline section of the Gloucester-Birmingham main line was created here in 1840 by the Birmingham & Gloucester Railway, the engine shed was situated on the east side of the main line whereas this siding and its attendant coal stage was provided for on the west side of the main line. A section of the coaling stage awning is visible on the right and as many as six locomotives were accommodated on the siding during busy periods of heavy traffic.

Besides the famous, or infamous, larger locomotives which have worked the Lickey incline, much of the work was done by the little engines allocated to Bromsgrove. During the LMS and early BR period the 3F 'Jinty' 0-6-0T's provided the motive power. Latterly, ex GWR 0-6-0PT's were also employed with equal acceptance. On my visit to the shed in September 1956 these three LMS built 'Jinties', 47425, 47276 and 47308 were outside having a Sunday break whilst others were inside the shed being maintained. Whereas one of the larger engines could manage most banking jobs alone, it was quite normal for three of these 0-6-0T's to be coupled together. Of course there were occasions when three 0-6-0T's and a large engine would be required. During the 1930's the LMS tended to keep six 0-6-0T, four 0-6-0's, a Sentinel (for shunting the adjacent wagon works) and the 0-10-0. In the mid 1940's there was a total of seven 0-6-0T, one 2F 0-6-0, one 0-10-0 and 2-6-4T No.2340. When Bromsgrove shed closed at the end of September 1964, No.47425 had already been scrapped after a previous transfer away to Aintree, No.47276 and 47308 had both been moved to Bath for a more sedate life. When the Western Region took over the running of the depot in 1958 they had already ousted some of the ex LMS engines and exchanged them for their own home-grown stock with Hawksworth 9400 Class 0-6-0PT Nos.8404 and 8410 rubbing shoulders with 'Jinty' No.47502. During the last summer of the depot's existence, the following former GWR locomotives were allocated, all 9400 Class 0-6-0PT Nos.8400, 8401, 8402, 8403, 8405, 8409, 8418, 9430, 9453, 9493.

Friday, 15th April 1955 - Nuneaton, an important junction on the West Coast main line north of Rugby was also home to an eight road engine shed with an allocation comprising approximately 60 to 85 locomotives at various periods. The locomotive stud, which was mainly made up of goods engines, included thirty or more 0-8-0's of LNWR origin and a couple of dozen 0-6-0 tender engines of Midland, Wessy and even Lanky origin - a real mixture. LMS types such as Fowler and Stanier 2-6-0's were around to handle to fast freight. Being situated as it was in a coal producing area, the composition of the locomotive allocation is understandable. The station itself was an important cross-roads for passenger traffic with lines radiating to Burton, Leicester, London, Coventry, Birmingham and northward to Crewe. A good number of the WCML express trains used to call here on their way to and from London Euston and Camden based 'Royal Scot' No.46170 BRITISH LEGION has just stopped with a Down express. No.46170 was the odd-one-out in the 'Scot' class and had started life as a high pressure compound locomotive built by the North British Locomotive Co. in 1929. Numbered 6399, it also carried the name FURY. It was rebuilt as a 3-cylinder simple and fitted with a No.2 boiler in 1935, at which time it was also taken into LMS stock. Note the steam pipe is different from the other 'Scots' in that it is not straight. The engine later acquired a double chimney and the name it wore through to withdrawal in 1962. During its experimental existence, the engine was allocated to Crewe North shed where its trials and tribulations could be monitored and any rectification could soon be sorted out at the adjacent works. After rebuilding it was transferred to Longsight in November 1935, returning to Crewe North in February 1937. October of the following year found it back in Manchester for a nine month stay after which it went back to Crewe again. It remained at 5A until July 1943 when, for some reason, it went on a month long loan to Leeds Holbeck shed. From there it went to Camden for a sixteen year residence broken only by a one month loan to Edge Hill in September 1945 and a similar period of loan to Crewe north in October 1958. In December 1959 it began a year long shed swap which saw it go to Preston, then Crewe North, Holyhead in June 1960, back to 5A in July, Camden in October and back to Crewe in November. Just two months before withdrawal in November 1962 it was transferred to Llandudno Junction shed. It then entered Crewe works, never to emerge again. One nameplate is now at the NRM.

Another 'Scot' appeared, this one, No.46143 THE SOUTH STAFFORDSHIRE REGIMENT, on a Down Liverpool working, 10.27 ex Nuneaton. This engine had been at Longsight since November 1952 and except for a six week loan to Holbeck in October, was to remain based in Manchester until November 1959 when it moved to Bushbury for a year. It went back to Manchester but to Trafford Park shed from where it worked expresses to St Pancras. In September 1962 it joined the band of fifteen unwanted and thoroughly worn out 'Royal Scots' which were transferred to the old Great Central route and worked from Annesley shed. Reprieve came in December 1963 when the scrapyard beckoned.

This Up train at Nuneaton is bathed in afternoon sun, or at least most of the engine is. The platform canopy on this side of the station during the afternoon cast a shadow on the wheels and motion of locomotives at this time of year. However, I was fortunate to capture this Kentish Town 'Jubilee', No.45598 BASUTOLAND (what fabulous names this class carried, all memorable as parts of the old empire, famous admirals, ships and sea battles.), en route back home after a major repair at Crewe. It has charge of a Euston bound train due away from Nuneaton at 12.54 pm. This engine started life at Carlisle Durranhill shed in February 1935 but returned to Crewe the following month. In June 1936 Edge Hill got it for a year before it moved permanently to the old Midland Division at Holbeck. After nine years in Leeds it went next to Saltley for four months prior to a prolonged stay at Kentish Town. Derby got it in November 1959 and two years later it went to Burton, no longer required for main line express passenger work. A move to Bank Hall shed in Liverpool during October 1964 never materialised, instead it was condemned and sold to T.W.Ward at Killamarsh.

Sunday 16th September 1956, a busy day indeed for me and my camera but worth the running around to catch scenes such as this little gathering inside the older of the Burton roundhouses. These BR Standard Cl.2 tank engines arrived at Burton, brand new, from Crewe works in 1953. No.84006 in August and 84007 in September. Another new member of the class, 84008 also arrived in September but alas it was not available for this picture - but this pair would do nicely. Taking over from the ex Midland 0-4-4T, the trio worked mainly on the 'Tutbury Jenny' push-pulls until withdrawal of those services left them without work and all three transferred to Wellingborough in 1959. The former Midland Railway engine shed at Burton consisted two roundhouses built at different periods, the first being built in 1870 and the later one in 1892. Throughout its life up to closure in September 1966, the depot had supported a mainly freight locomotive allocation with some passenger tanks or 4-4-0's to look after the local passenger services. In the summer of 1935, out of a total allocation of 114 engines, some seventy-five of them were 0-6-0 tender engines. In 1944 the numbers were somewhat similar although six of those comprised Southern Railway locomotives on loan for the duration of the war.

The LMS Fowler 'Crab' first came into production in 1926 but the class was not represented at Burton until the middle of the 1930's when at least three of them were allocated: 2767, 2768 and 2898. No.42922, seen here in September 1956, was one of fourteen allocated by the end of the 1950's. Also included in that number were the five Reidinger rotary cam poppet valve fitted engines: 42818, 42822, 42824, 42825 and 42829 which were all concentrated here by the end of that decade. All five of them were withdrawn in the early summer of 1962.

The LMS Standard Cl.4 0-6-0 tender engine class comprised 575 locomotives numbered from 4027 to 4606. Construction started in 1924 and with over five hundred in traffic by 1928 it ceased only to start up again some nine years later when fifteen more engines were built. In 1939 the design was called upon yet again to provide another thirty engines, the last of which, Nos.4605 and 4606 emerged from Derby in 1941. Burton's No.44599, seen here on 8th July 1956, was amongst four of the class which the shed acquired from the batch built in 1940. Originally these wartime built locomotives were to receive the new 4,000 gallon tenders built with them but instead their tenders went to 'Jubilee' class engines which had been attached to 3,500 gallon tenders since new. Thereafter, the 0-6-0's received the second-hand 3,500 gallon tenders from the 5XP's as here. This particular tender (No.4565) is one of the ten 3,500 gallon examples with high straight sides having a seven ton coal capacity The 4F has charge of a Permanent Way train, complete with crane, on the main line past the shed - after all it is a Sunday.

Deeley 0F 0-4-0T No.41536 was a long time resident of Burton shed and was not the only one its type allocated. In 1945 three of the class, 1530, 1535 and 1536, found employment in the local brewery yards where their short wheelbase was ideal for working through the exceptionally tight radius curves in the trackwork. Besides these engines, two ex Midland 0-4-0 saddletanks of an earlier vintage shared the brewery duties. No.41536, seen on 16th September 1956, propped up on an accommodation bogie outside the wheel drop shed *(above)*, and in frontal pose *(opposite)* was still active around the breweries - wheels permitting, as was sister engine 41532. By this date No.1530 had been scrapped along with the ex MR saddletanks. These are the type of views which modellers appreciate, showing detail not normally visible. The older No.1 roundhouse looms behind the 0-4-0T whilst on the right is the ornate sand drying house.

On the 8th July 1956 ex Lancashire & Yorkshire 0-4-0ST No.51235 was hogging the wheel drop. Although wearing a 17A Derby shed plate, the tiny 0-4-0 was on Burton's 'books' during the 1940's but now Derby had acquired it for whatever reason. During the 1930's, Burton shed had housed two of the L&Y saddletanks (besides two ex Lanky Barton-Wright 0-6-0 tender engines). In WW2 the ex Caledonian 0-4-0ST No.16020 joined the other four-coupled engines on the brewery turns. One can understand a brewery job in Burton attracting residents of Derby and Salford but Glasgow - interesting times for all. Amongst the last of the small engines working from Burton were the LMS Kitson built 0-4-0ST's, of the 47XXX series, which performed around the town during the latter days of steam but by 1964 branch closures were taking place with the inevitable redundancies.

The somewhat distinguished facade of Ashby-de-la-Zouch station in April 1956. The stonework was in need of a clean but otherwise, at first appearance, this could have been the ground floor section of a local stately home. The ornate carving of the stone, especially around the entrance portico, leaves one to believe that whoever commissioned this building had a grand vision for the town. Ashby stood at the junction of the line from Burton and the one from Derby which continued to Leicester through Coalville. The area was rich in coal reserves with numerous mines served by the Midland Railway. Perhaps it was the mine owners who had something to do with the grandiose frontage of this station but whoever was behind the original scheme it left an impressive building which added to the richness of BR property in the 1950's.

Desford station, seen on 14th April 1956, was the junction of the Leicester West Bridge branch where it met the Burton to Leicester line. The two separate levels in the platform indicate the two different periods in the life of this station. The lower level probably dates from about 1832 when the Leicester & Swannington Rly opened as far as Bagworth. The high level platform dates from the arrival of the Midland in 1849 when they opened the direct route from their main line at Leicester to connect with Burton-upon-Trent. It was then that Desford became the junction for the West Bridge branch.

Ratby was the first intermediate station between Desford and West Bridge, a single platform sufficing throughout its long though less than glorious history which came to an end in September 1928 when passenger services on the branch were withdrawn. Although the derelict wooden buildings appear to lack any permanence, they do show some individuality in their architectural style with every window and doorway being 'arched'. The span of the small canopy is somewhat parsimonious as to afford little if any cover from inclement weather. On the other hand, the platform seems over generous in length and those copings would not wear out in a thousand years or more.

Glenfield was the penultimate station before West Bridge. The station building was a virtual copy of the one at Ratby, even down to the combined roof and overhanging canopy. The siding served a coal merchant and a century of spilt coal dust has raised the ground so that it was, by April 1956, level with the top of the rail. Why the station nameboard was still prominent after nearly thirty years of obscurity, I have no idea but at least it helps to identify the place.

The western end of the 'mile and a bit and dead straight' (1796 yards actually) Glenfield tunnel with the eastern end just visible in April 1956. Though the passenger services had long been history on this branch line, the goods facility at West Bridge required daily trip working by locomotives from Coalville engine shed to keep the goods flowing. The one 'thorn in the side' in keeping the branch open was this horseshoe profiled tunnel which had such limited clearance it could only accommodate locomotives with cut-down cabs. It is reputed to have no refuges for platelayers working in the tunnel during operating periods so how they operated under such conditions!!!

Leicester West Bridge terminus had a large goods yard but the passenger facilities consisted this one platform with associated passenger and staff accommodation. At least the building here is a more substantial brick structure although there does not appear to be any signs of a canopy. Note that a proper fireplace has been installed here whereas Ratby and Glenfield stations made do with pot-bellied stoves or something similar. Are they black-out shutters alongside the waiting room windows? Besides the goods and passenger facilities, West Bridge terminus could also boast a one road brick built engine shed where the pilot and branch engine could house themselves overnight. However, the LMS must have looked upon the shed as Midland extravagance because in 1926, after a through assessment of the company assets, they closed the place. Demolition of that facility did not happen straight away (the closed stations are testament to that) and it was used whenever necessary until WW2.

West Bridge yard, Leicester, 14th April 1956 with ex Midland Johnson 2F No.58246 in steam and working the branch. Some six of so years later, the last of the Johnson Cl.2F 0-6-0s working on British Railways, Nos.58143 (ex Saltley), 58148 (ex Bushbury), and 58182 (ex Barrow), were all concentrated at Coalville shed for working the West Bridge branch which they did until the end of 1963 when the first of two BR Standard Cl.2 2-6-0 tender engines, 78013, arrived in December. Until 78013 was joined by 78028 in the following January, one of the 2F's, the eighty-eight year old No.58182, lingered on as a stand-by (at that time, January 1964, it was the oldest running locomotive on BR). Crewe works had altered both Standards by cutting back and lowering the corners of the cab roof to allow running through Glenfield tunnel; the total cost is reputed as being £600. Both the BR Standards transferred to Leicester Midland shed in September and when the West Bridge branch closed in May 1966, Nos.78013 and 78028, along with two other unmodified class members moved to Toton for storage in June, finally being officially transferred to that depot in July. The BR 2-6-0's were withdrawn early the following year after moving to the last stronghold of BR steam - Lancashire.

Amongst the numerous prototype diesel locomotives 'trialed' by British Railways during the 1950's was this Bo-Bo diesel electric built by the North British Locomotive Co. in 1950. Ordered by the LMS in 1946, the NBL Co. eventually got round to building it in 1949-50, with BR then obliged to take it off their hands. Numbered 10800, it certainly had North American design influence built in. Initially allocated to Willesden motive power depot and then Bletchley, the black livered locomotive 'toured' the Region for various trials during its nine years of 'acceptance'. It even worked on the Southern for a while in 1952 but was sent back to the LMR. Plaistow of all places had it for a three month period then Rugby tried it. Here at Leicester (London Road) in April 1955 it is engaged in passenger working's between Birmingham (New Street), Cambridge and Norwich. The 827 h.p. 16-cylinder Paxman diesel engine produced enough power to give the locomotive a maximum speed of 70 m.p.h., so it was ideal for stopping and semi-fast passenger services. However, 10800 did not impress the authorities and in 1959 it was laid up never to work again for BR. Brush Traction purchased the locomotive and between 1962 and 1964 modified it as a testing unit for the development of a.c. traction equipment. It even got a new Maybach engine. It did venture out onto the main line for trials from the Brush works at Loughborough but never went into revenue service. Reputedly named HAWK by Brush, it was never seem carrying such a name although it kept its original numerical designation. It was finally scrapped in 1976.

Leicester (Belgrave Road) station had six platform faces and when opened for business in 1882 the GNR must have been supremely confident of its future because they covered the platforms with two rather grand arched roofs. The front entrance was no slum either with brick built offices above passenger facilities reached via a covered roadway. However, Belgrave Road did not quite live up to those expectations and regular passenger services ceased in April 1957. Prior to that, local services were run to Grantham, Newark, Nottingham, Peterborough, with summer services to the Lincolnshire coast. The latter still used the station at weekends up until 1962 when all passenger facilities were withdrawn. Prior to the local services being cut, J6 No.64235, standing at the old platform 5 in 1953, heads a midday working to Grantham consisting of just two coaches. *Authors collection.*

Its summer in Leicester and its raining. On 22nd August 1953, Colwick J11 No.64438 has just arrived at Belgrave Road station with a stopping service from Nottingham (Victoria). The 0-6-0 will uncouple, draw forward, run round its train and makes its way to the depot for turning prior to reversing onto its two-coach train and awaiting the signal for the journey back to Nottingham. Even though this was the only platform in use at this period, the J11 had plenty of time to carry out the necessary manoeuvres, such was the intervals between services. Note that platforms 1, 2 and 3 on the left have been taken out of passenger use by means of erecting a wooden barrier along the entire length of platform 3 and 4. No.4 was used occasionally but No.5 was the only platform face required normally. Even in the early 1950's 'the writing was on the wall' for this station. Platform No.6 on the right was being used to stable what appears to be a very interesting collection of coaching stock at this time; indeed, the whole station area became a dumping ground for ancient and redundant coaching stock.

Ivatt/Gresley J6 No.64252, of Retford GN shed, drifts through Melton Mowbray North on its way to Leicester with a Class A goods train on the morning of Tuesday 6th September 1955. The goods facilities at this station were very similar to those offered at the former Midland station, even down to the same lifting capacity of the yard crane - 5 tons. On the north side of the line can be seen the livestock loading platform, now taken over for timber and construction materials storage, whilst on this side stood the large goods warehouse. The signalbox, perched atop its own gantry, was built in 1914 and replaced the two original boxes which stood at either end of the goods yard on opposite sides of the line. The new box had a commanding view of the main line as it swept down from the north in a curve which put it onto a west/east axis as it passed through the station. Once clear of the station precincts, the line curved southwards to regain its original alignment. Pre-war, this line could boast up to ten LNER passenger trains daily with an equal number run by the LMS. Goods train frequency was slightly less. This GN/LNW Joint line, which opened fully in 1879, was useful in many ways for both concerns, especially as a through route between main centres but the wayside stations on the route never did live up to supplying the expected traffic envisaged by Victorian optimism. Up to 1914 it was possible to board a LNWR carriage at Nottingham (London Road Low Level) and travel to London (Euston) without having to change, however, the privilege took nearly four hours but Melton North was one of the intermediate stations. At that time the Midland were offering a two hour, twelve minute timing from Nottingham on their train to St Pancras via Melton Mowbray. Therefore, until the First World War, the town enjoyed services to London by both routes. Melton Mowbray North closed as a passenger station in December 1953, note the weeds already flexing their muscles, whilst the goods facility was given up in May 1964. Now redundant, the line was abandoned, such duplication and extravagance could not be tolerated in the Beeching era. So, like the age of steam this Joint line ran its course and was then given up. Demolition of the railway facilities started with a vengeance in 1970 and today this same site is occupied by a large retail outlet.

Ivatt Cl.4 No.43110, of South Lynn shed, leaves Melton Mowbray on its way back to the M&GN, via Bourne and Spalding, with a train from Nottingham on the last day of May, 1955. Note the tablet catcher in the recess on the tender of the 2-6-0. Since new from Doncaster works in June 1951, and except for a two month loan in the summer of 1957, this engine was allocated to South Lynn shed until the closure of the Midland & Great Northern system. Its final depot was Boston from where it worked until being condemned in December 1963. Melton Mowbray, population 9,187 in 1927, and 105 miles from London had a typical Midland station, complete with lattice girder footbridge. Happily, the station is still operational in 2005 though there is no longer a direct service to London after the curtailment of the Nottingham trains in the late 1960's. On the south western outskirts of the town, where the Midland's former Nottingham and Leicester routes diverged (Melton Junction), the ex Great Northern and London & North Western Railway Joint line passed over the two lines by way of overbridges and it was at this point where a spur, known as Sysonby curve, once connected for a short period in the 1880's, the Joint line with the Midland line.

*(opposite)* A Joint line trespass notice at Melton Mowbray, 6th September 1955. Its apparent lean perhaps reflecting the fortunes of this route.

Kentish Town 'Jubilee' No.45557 NEW BRUNSWICK heads through Melton Mowbray towards Nottingham (Midland) with a Leeds (City) bound train from St Pancras on 31st May 1955. Just over fourteen years later the Midland route from Nottingham would be closed as another Beeching 'measure'. However, the run down to closure had started in earnest in 1966 when only one weekday Nottingham-London return service came through Melton. Not only did Melton lose its direct services to London but Nottingham suffered too because all 'through' trains now had to reverse in Nottingham (Midland) to regain the main line with the resultant extended timings on long distance services which plagued the city, and BR until recent times.

*(opposite)* Think of the LMS Garratts and you think of Toton, their home for thirty-two years; at least for some of them. Toton was, however, associated with the class for all that time and, at one time or another, all thirty-three members of the class have been allocated to the shed. Hasland was the next depot, in terms of how many 2-6-0+0-6-2's had been allocated over the years, where these monsters found rest and twenty-two of them made up the number. Wellingborough, half way down the line to London, comes a close third with nineteen on the books at various times. Westhouses had a meagre three but joined the band of only five depots which looked after them. Finally, Cricklewood, where they mainly worked to anyway, had two new members of the class allocated in the early days. On Tuesday 31st May 1955, Garratt No.47974 heads a northbound empty mineral train into Melton Mowbray station and is passing under the road bridge from where I took a couple of the previous views. By this date only one of this class had been withdrawn but the wheels for their demise were in motion and within a couple of years all but one would have been cut up at Crewe works. The odd one out, No.47985, had been caught in the middle of an ASLEF dispute whilst en route to Crewe so Derby works, where it was dumped at the start of the strike, promptly set about it with cutting torches and that was that. All the rest made it to Crewe. None were preserved as they were regarded as something of a nuisance by BR rather than an asset. The engines were certainly dealt with quickly once condemned and within days, if not already at Crewe, they were dragged there and cut up straight away. No.47974 still had another twelve months of work ahead of it before the call came from Crewe.

From virtually the same position on the A606 roadbridge as explained on page 50, but on the 6th September of that same year, I caught Stanier Cl.5 No.44848 of Millhouses shed, on a Sheffield (Midland) to London (St Pancras) train. At Saxby Junction this train would diverge southwards heading for Corby and bypassing Leicester. Note the self weighing tender (probably No.10590) attached to 44848. This was one of four used with this class and had only recently been put with this engine. Since emerging from Crewe in November 1944, No.44848 spent eighteen years on the former LMS Midland Division, starting at Holbeck. During the first month of BR it moved to Saltley then ten months later to Derby. Before moving on to Millhouses in September 1953, it went on loan to Kingmoor for a few weeks. Derby got it back in October 1955 and kept hold of it until January 1959 when Leicester acquired it. Three years later No.44848 moved across town to the ex GC shed from where it plied the GC main line. Proceeding deeper into GC territory it moved to Annesley in July 1964 and when that place closed in January 1966 Colwick had it for three months. Its final depot was Rose Grove where, in February 1968, it was withdrawn. It was purchased for scrap by Cohen's whose Kettering yard was not too far from this spot.

Tallington on the East Coast Main Line was situated approximately seven miles north of Peterborough. At this point the A16 trunk road crossed the line via a level crossing, one of the few still in situ on this busy main line at that time. On 13th May 1956 the former Great Northern station was still in business but only just because in 1959 it would be closed as one of the pre-Beeching casualties. Looking from the footbridge we can see New England based J6 No.64246 working tender first with an ancient six-wheel coach which was part of the New England breakdown train. Note the modifications on the roof of the coach where additional natural lighting has been added.

A St Pancras to Leeds (City), via Melton Mowbray, working is brought into Nottingham (Midlands) station by 'Jubilee' No.45639 RALEIGH, on Monday 11th April 1955. This engine was based at Holbeck, transferred there from Nottingham in July 1951 after it spent just a month at 16A, its only period of allocation to Nottingham. Its name would have been appropriate for the city but the railway authorities do not see such things in the same sentimental light as enthusiats. No.45639's time on the Midland Division started at Kentish Town in septmeber 1938 and ending at the Leeds shed in September 1963 when the famous Admiral was withdrawn.

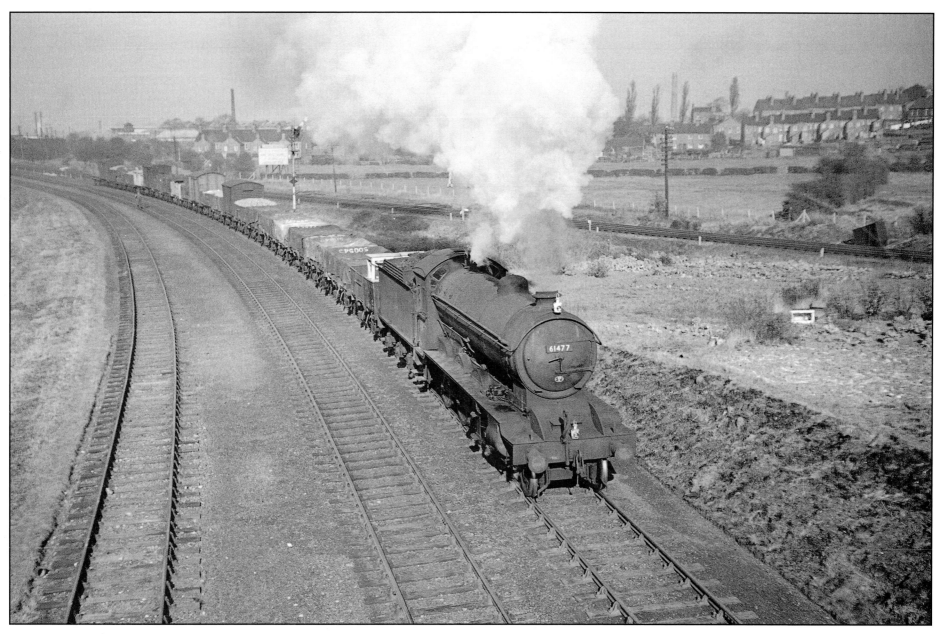

B16 No.61477 leaves Newark and the ECML behind as it branches off towards Bottesford with a Colwick bound freight on 31st October 1955. The nine mile long branch line to Bottesford was opened in 1878 and was a fairly easy route for engines with no severe gradients and plenty of level running. In 1970 the branch was singled and flat bottomed rails were installed to upgrade the route which was still serving a cement works and a gypsum factory. The only passenger station on the route, Cotham, had closed in September 1939 whilst the adjoining goods yard lasted until February 1964. However, closure of the whole line came in April 1987 as, by then, the traffic was a shadow of previous times and the track bed was apparently in urgent need of renewal. Besides, an alternative was available via the old Midland line from Nottingham to Newark. The B16 was York based and a regular performer on this traffic. This engine should have become No.61408 but it was amongst the ten early B16's (1400-1409) which were renumbered 61469 to 61478 in December 1949 to make their numbers available for new Thompson B1's which were then coming into traffic. No.1408 had not received its BR number at the time but seven of the other affected engines had. Condemned in February 1960, No.61477 was cut up at Darlington.

A classic shot of an A3 speeding south on the ECML shortly after leaving Newark behind. The location is Newark Junction in 1957 and No.60065 KNIGHT OF THISTLE is working a Newcastle-King's Cross express as far as Grantham where it will detach and hand the train over to a 'Top shed' engine. Rebuilt from an A10 in March 1947, the A3 worked from sheds situated on the southern stretch of the ECML and on this date was allocated to Grantham shed. It was amongst the last of the active Eastern Region based A3's and was not condemned until the end of June 1964. It was sold for scrap to a Norwich scrapyard during the following August.

Virtually brand new English Electric Type 4 diesel-electric D207 has charge of an Up express at Newark in August 1958. The summer of 1958 saw the introduction of this class onto the ECML but at the time there was only a handful of them and so they were hardly noticed. Five of the type (D201, and D206 to D209) were allocated to temporary accommodation at Hornsey engine shed in 1958 and until further members of the class started arriving at Gateshead in late 1959, they were basically the sole main line diesel power available for express passenger work on the ECML. Of course the Eastern Region authorities were awaiting the arrival of the 'Deltics' in early 1961 to take over the prestigious named trains and until then the Gresley and Peppercorn Pacifics would suffice. A new diesel depot was being built at Finsbury Park in London but that too would not be ready until early 1960 and so these 'pioneer' diesel locomotives had to make do.

Slowing for the Newark station stop, Peppercorn A1 No.60149 AMADIS drifts under the roadbridge at the north end of the station with an Up express in the summer of 1957. The new roadbridge, which replaced a level crossing, was an ideal vantage point to observe and photograph the virtual non-stop procession of trains on this section of the ECML. The maltings on the left also feature in the previous view of D207 but it is now possible to see the wagon turntable which had been put in by the GNR to service these particular premises which were an important component of the local economy. Note the stop blocks between the turntable and the Down main and just behind the temporary speed restriction sign - the clearance is minimal and I should imagine that such a 'set-up' would not be allowed today. The A1 was based at King's Cross shed and on this date was approximately half way through its short life.

En route to its home depot after a 'General' overhaul at Doncaster works, Ivatt LMS Class 4F 2-6-0 No.43161 passes through Newark on 13th October 1955. Home was Yarmouth Beach shed on the Midland & Great Northern Joint line and No.43161 was one of twenty of its class sent new to the M&GN in 1952. In 1959, with the complete closure of the M&GN system, the 2-6-0 moved to Norwich Thorpe shed but transferred to Staveley GC shed in December 1960. Grimesthorpe got it two months later and then in August 1961 it went to Colwick. Its final shed was Staveley Barrow Hill where it transferred to in March 1963. The inevitable end came in June 1965 after which it was sold for scrap, less than thirteen years old.

Dukeries Junction, Tuxford, Nottinghamshire, was the point where the Lancashire, Derbyshire & East Coast Railway crossed the Great Northern main line by this overbridge. The station on the bridge was known as Dukeries Junction and was the LD&EC section of a joint station which closed to passengers in 1950 along with its former GN counterpart on the lower level. In this 3rd June 1956 view the island platform station is looking the worse for wear and would soon be demolished. Behind the camera stood the three road engine shed known until closure in February 1959 as Tuxford. Beyond that, a little further to the west was the former locomotive works of the LD&ECR also known as Tuxford but which ceased to repair locomotives shortly after Grouping when wagon repair became the main occupation. The bridge here is still in situ serving the occasional Merry-Go-Round coal trains which run from Thoresby Colliery to High Marnham power station.

To find an ex Great Eastern J67 0-6-0T at Retford engine shed in 1956 was not that unusual because by now these little, yet useful, engines had spread all over the former LNER system like a rash. Retford had at least two of them at this time; Doncaster had a number also, so did Trafford Park and other sheds on the exCLC system, not to mention those which had resided in Scotland since the 1920's. Anyway No.68519 was by now classified J69 Part 2 since it was rebuilt so during a 'General' overhaul at Stratford in April 1950. At the time it was a Stratford based engine but on 6th November 1955 it broke out and got as far as New England. Hiding out there for a month, it escaped up the ECML as far as Retford on 4th December. No.68520 joined it two weeks later but had come from Stratford via Mexborough and Doncaster. When this photograph of 68519 was captured on 6th March 1956 it had been two years since a works visit and it shows somewhat. Obviously requiring attention of one form or another, including a new front left spectacle plate, the little engine is suspended between timber balks and the sheerlegs hoist. Condemned in August 1958, the J69/2 was replaced by others of its ilk and even in 1960 there were still three of the class allocated to Retford.

The more usual inhabitants of Retford in March 1956 included these two Thompson B1's, Nos.61266 of Doncaster shed and resident 61211 which was to spend the whole of its life allocated to the depot until withdrawn at Doncaster works and cut up there in November 1962. No.61211 had recently been through the shops at Doncaster works for a 'General' overhaul and would manage two more such repairs before being condemned. No.61266, another North British Loco. Co. built engine, was to have an even short active life than its Retford cousin. It was condemned in September 1962 at Darnall shed and sold for scrap in January 1963. This is the yard of the former GN shed which had undergone rebuilding a couple of years before. The ex Great Central shed (Thrumpton), situated to the east of the main line and was under the charge of the same Shedmaster, had also been rebuilt in early BR days. Neither of the engine sheds here lasted long enough to see the end of steam on the Eastern Region.

I have included this picture I took at Frodingham on 6th March 1956 of a 1925 built Pullman car. Other than the date of construction, the fact it was a twelve-wheeler and it was a Brake First, I know little else about it. Why it was dumped at Frodingham shed in the first place nor when was it last in revenue service and on which lines it worked, I know nothing. Finally, what happened to it?

*(opposite)* Before Doncaster station was rebuilt with a more open aspect by British Railways, this is what the place looked like when viewed from the footbridge linking the Up and Down platforms. The date is 30th September 1956 and working along the Up main is Grantham based A3 No.60065 KNIGHT OF THISTLE with a London train. On the Up platform is a B1 with another southbound working whilst the Down platform canopy conceals a northbound train. Note that the original glass panels have long gone from the two canopies spanning the platform lines.

*(right)* Inside the 'Plant' at Doncaster on 6th March 1956 was the unique W1 class No.60700 with 'Not To Be Moved' signs attached to lamp irons at both front and back. Since its derailment at Westwood Junction, Peterborough on 1st September 1955, the 4-6-4 had undergone a three month 'General' overhaul which took it up to Christmas 1955 but since then it had done little work as can be seen from its generally 'smart' appearance on this date. Rebuilt in November 1937 from the LNER Hush-Hush No.10000, No.60700 was allocated to King's Cross shed for much of the time up to October 1953 when it transferred to Doncaster shed. Note the bulge of the cylinders compared with the footplate width. When side skirting was first fitted to this engine that bulge was even more noticeable. Most of its time at Doncaster shed saw it working London expresses but towards he end of its life it was not adverse to working stopping trains to both Leeds and Sheffield. Being a one-off in any mechanical environment is a precarious existence and it is amazing that the big W1 lasted as long as it did before it went for scrap in 1959.

At an earlier date, 6th April 1955, the southern end of the station looks little different. However, the unusual motive power combination of Thompson L1 No.67765 based at Hull Botanic Gardens shed and D20 No.62384, of Selby shed, add some interest. The train which they are heading may well have been an Up main line Pacific working on which the locomotive has failed somewhere near Selby. The L1 would have been called upon because it was in the area and the 4-4-0 was perhaps station pilot at Selby. I cannot remember the exact circumstances but the train has stopped on the Up main line at Doncaster for the reason of changing to more suitable motive power such as the Doncaster main line pilot, a Thompson A2. Although the L1 worked for another seven years, mainly at sheds in the north-east, the D20 was on its last legs and only four months away from condemnation. This particular exploit was probably its last major working in its forty-eight year life prior to withdrawal.

V2 No.60881 at Doncaster works in October 1956, its final visit to that place before all V2 maintenance was transferred to Darlington works. This picture throws up a few interesting points. The engine has just undergone a 'General' overhaul and has been painted in black lined livery; by December 1956 it was decreed that all V2 repaints would be done in lined Brunswick green as befitted such a locomotive. Note that the lining along the edge of the running plate continues vertically where it meets the bufferbeam. This was a Doncaster trait and was not followed by Darlington. No.60881 still has its original one piece monobloc cylinders but was to be one of the seventy-two V2's fitted with three separate cylinders. That was carried out during its next 'General' at Darlington in 1958. Although this engine had spent most of its life working from Doncaster shed from new in October 1940. It was allocated to Sheffield (Neepsend) and then Sheffield (Darnall) for the period from February 1941 to April 1947. One of only twenty-five V2's built by Doncaster works, No.60881 was appropriately cut up there in December 1963.

Virtually every weekday afternoon a procession of repaired locomotives would leave the works at Doncaster and be towed to Carr engine shed for lighting up and eventual road testing. On one particular sunny afternoon in May 1957 Doncaster O2 No.63969 has the job of hauling four 'dead' ex works engines and is passing through the station on the Up main. K3 No.61834 had just undergone a 'General' overhaul and repaint and has a week of running-in before being released back to its home shed at Stratford. The first Pacific is believed to be A1 No.60120 KITTIWAKE finishing a 'Heavy Intermediate' repair whilst the other is Peppercorn A2 No.60527 SUN CHARIOT, another repainted engine after a 'General'. Bringing up the rear is one of the Ivatt LMS designed 2-6-0's which Doncaster 'Plant' was responsible for maintaining after building fifty of them between 1950 and 1952. Both the repainted locomotives carry the newly introduced BR crest which had replaced the 'lion & wheel' emblem. Note that by now the original canopy which straddled the Up platform road has been replaced by a modern cantilever canopy as part of the station modernisation at this time. The canopy on the Down side is in the process of removal and has already lost much of its original length. *Authors collection.*

Of the three railway stations which Chesterfield could once boast, the Midland Railway establishment was probably the worse placed for the town centre but today it is the only survivor of the original trio. The first Midland station was sited even further from the centre of town but in 1870 a new station was built on the present site. In March 1956 this was the facade of that former MR station, appropriately named Midland in its BR guise. Except for the BR enamel nameboard, the frontage in this view is little changed from its condition at the turn of the century. However, things were bound to change and during the period from 1963 to 1965, the station was rebuilt. Not content with that design, BR decided that a revamp was required thirty years later and that also went ahead so that the 2005 station is far removed, in every way, from the first station of 1840.

On a damp 3rd March 1956, the train side of Chesterfield station had the Up and Down main lines, a couple of bay platforms and independent goods lines. Bristol Barrow Road 'Jubilee' No.45662 KEMPENFELT has just started an Up express bound for Bristol Temple Meads and is having trouble finding its feet. One of only ten 'Jubilees' built at Derby, this engine was allocated to Bristol when new in December 1934, but by the following February it was transferred to Kentish Town for a twelve year stint which included a month on loan to Derby shed in October 1944. When Barrow Road got it back in November 1947 it stayed this time for fourteen years becoming a Western Region engine when the old Midland engine sheds in the West of England came under Paddington control in the 1950's. 45662's transfer away from Bristol in September 1961 naturally took it to another WR shed but one with LMS connections - Shrewsbury. When withdrawal came, in November 1962, Crewe works efficiently carried out the deed and 45662 was no more.

When the Manchester, Sheffield & Lincolnshire Railway constructed their loop line through the centre of Chesterfield in 1892, they built this wooden facility on the road bridge spanning their main line. In order to keep costs down, timber was the cheapest construction material although some embellishments such as the wrought iron 'crown' above the booking hall were permitted. Timber it may have been, the building certainly weathered quite well as witness this March 1956 view of the facade. This station was nearer to the town centre and to distinguish the place from the Midland and LD&ECR premises, the name Central was applied in 1907. The Great Central main line expresses between Manchester and London thundered along the main line to the east by-passing Chesterfield, so the town had to make do with the GCR stopping services between Sheffield and Nottingham. Although this section of the former GC main line did not close until 1966, the station itself closed in 1963 and all trace was swept away during a town centre 'road improvement' scheme.

Chesterfield's third station, the last one built, the largest, and certainly the most impressive, was the one erected in 1897 by the Lancashire, Derbyshire & East Coast Railway at the Market Place. This station was situated on the west side of the town, nearer to LD&ECR's intended, though never attained, destination. Behind the facade were four terminal platforms built with an optimistic future in the mind of the developers. Although passenger services were withdrawn from the station in 1951, because of a tunnel collapse, BR maintained offices and car parking when this view was captured on Saturday 3rd March 1956. Apparently the building is still in use although the station platforms are long gone.

Horn's Bridge, Chesterfield, 3rd March 1956. The only place in Chesterfield where all three of the railway companies came together, albeit at different elevations, was at Horns Bridge. This view, showing about a half of the impressive structure, with the former MS&L route at the lower level, is looking south. A brakevan is left protecting the shunting movement on the main line ahead where a train is being pushed into the adjacent private siding. The LD&EC line to Tuxford and Lincoln crossed over the bridge as a J11 No.64296 is doing now with a load of empty coal wagons. The Midland main line, at a level approximately halfway between those of the MS&L and the LD&EC, was off picture to the right on its own embankment. Built in 1897, the seven hundred foot long structure not only passed over the two railways, it also went over two main roads and the River Rother some sixty-three feet below. Not quite reaching its centenary, this bridge was demolished in 1984, its full potential never realised. Of the three railway lines only the oldest route, that of the MR, remains and everything else has given way to the motor car.

The Cromford & High Peak line offered some interesting views for the enthusiast and photographer alike and Cromford end of Sheep Pasture incline especially was amongst its many gems. The steepness of this gradient, which averaged about 1 in 8, can be appreciated by looking at the horizontal bridge abutment on the right. In order to keep the wire guides in gauge, the guides themselves are set in the centre, then offset to the right and inclined, moving towards the middle of the track until they are then up against the opposite rail and then moving across the track once again to take up a central position once the track has straightened out. On the other side of the bridge was the foot of the incline where the railway levelled out and met the Manchester-Derby main line. To get a train up this incline, in the Down direction, took about nine minutes for the 580 yards during which the elevation changed just over 200 feet. Trains coming down, in the Up direction, took a minute longer.

The tonnage of coal which has trundled through the Midland's Erewash valley on the main line to Toton yard must equate to more than a billion tons during the age of steam alone. The flow from the Derbyshire and Nottinghamshire collieries was phenomennal to say the least and, industrial action apart, it was a six day a week operation for the railway with staging and concentration yards from Chesterfield to Stanton Gate. Engine sheds also marked the route, Hasland, Westhouses, Toton and of course those not quite on the valley route but which fed onto the main line with their local pit's production. Ex MR Fowler 4F No.43845 epitomised the long time motive power on this route, the 0-6-0 tender engine. Here at Trowell, on a summer evening in 1957, the forty-year-old locomotive is drifting down to Toton with a heavy train of industrial coal.

Winter sunshine, when it appears, can be quite intense and ideal for photography. On Saturday 31st March 1956, the dales of the southern Peak District were bathed in glorious sunlight and from the Down platform of Matlock Bath station I caught 'Jubilee' No.45614 LEEWARD ISLANDS blasting through with an early afternoon Manchester (Central) to London (St Pancras) express. At the time of the photograph, this engine was allocated to Kentish Town engine shed, a depot where it had first arrived in January 1935 after transfer from Camden. In March 1940 it was on loan to Toton for a couple of months but the reason why is shrouded in wartime secrecy. This was a regular duty and therefore very familiar territory for 45614 and would be until May 1959 when it moved to the old Central Division at Newton Heath shed to help out with the summer season traffic in the Manchester area. Returning to London at the end of the 1959 Summer WTT, the 'Jubilee' had another stint in Manchester during February 1960 but this time at Trafford Park shed, doing just what it did from Kentish Town, working the Manchester-London services. In December 1961, with the 'Peaks' now well and truly in charge of the main line services on the Midland Lines, No.45614 went to Derby and from there, in an effort to find suitable work, it moved to Buxton in April 1962 just in time to endure one of the coldest winters on record. It escaped to Derby in January 1963 and for another year it carried out any duty thrown at it in between bouts of storage. In January 1964 it was condemned and shortly afterwards it was purchased for scrap by Albert Looms at nearby Spondon.

Shortly after LEEWARD ISLANDS had passed through, this Kirkby-in-Ashfield based Stanier 8F, No.48009, approached rapidly from the north with an express freight. One of the pioneer LMS Crewe built 2-8-0's, 48009 went new in 1935 to Willesden shed but was soon afterwards transferred to the Midland Division at Toton. From there it went to Wellingborough in September 1936 but returned to Toton during the war. It final move was to Kirkby-in-Ashfield in June 1943 from where it worked up to withdrawal in December 1962. This was the only 8F condemned in 1962 and essentially the first to be withdrawn other than for accident damage or military use. For whatever reason 48009 was condemned, it must have been severe because serious inroads into the class did not start until 1964. Derby works cut up the 2-8-0 in January 1963.

Rowsley 4F No.44564 takes the North Junction at Ambergate during the morning of the last day of March 1956 with a short goods working. The bright sunshine was a reminder of what was to come during the following months but the bitter easterly wind kept our enthusiasm checked.

In 1956 Derby locomotive works was still the centre of engineering excellence that it had been for a century. New locomotives building during the year included this 350 h.p. diesel electric shunter of a type which Derby built in their hundreds during the latter days of the LMS and certainly during the BR years of 'Modernisation'. On Sunday, 8th July 1956, No.13261, resplendant in green livery, was one of a few brand new examples waiting around the works to be called into traffic. What became the BR Class 08, these 0-6-0 DE shunters could be found in all the far flung corners of Britain and everywhere else in between. This engine was off to South Wales, Llanelly to be exact. In September 1960 it became D3261 but never got its 08 number, being withdrawn from Cardiff's Canton depot in December 1972. For a member of this very large class it had a relatively short working life but perhaps that helped to give it a new lease of life in preservation.

*(opposite)* Inside the shops at Derby, amongst the new builds on that July 1956 Sunday, one of the diesel 'old timers' was having some attention to its engine. 12001 was one of the Hawthorn Leslie 0-6-0 DE shunters built for the LMS in September 1936 and numbered 7076. It worked all of its life from Crewe South shed where many of those early diesels found favour in the large and busy yards. 7076 got its BR number in September 1949 and worked until February 1962 when it was withdrawn and then cut up at Horwich works in the following May. During WW2 this locomotive had a couple of short spells with the War Department but most of the conflict was spent with the LMS at Crewe.

Sister engine 12002, another Hawthorn Leslie product but from April 1934, was in Derby works on the 8th July 1956 for a more serious problem - condemnation. Withdrawn the previous month, the locomotive has been stripped of any useful parts, including the middle set of wheels. This locomotive was on loan to the LMS as a demonstration model from the engine maker English Electric until the railway company purchased in 1936 and numbered it No.7079 in their growing diesel fleet. Renumbered 12002 by BR in September 1949, this was another life long Crewe South resident. It was cut up by Derby in September.

Ironically Derby was still building steam locomotives whilst building, repairing and scrapping diesels. Here in the erecting shop on Sunday 8th July 1956, and going through the last phases of fitting out whilst at the same time receiving its first coats of paint, was one of the Caprotti examples of the BR Standard Class 5, No.73126 which went into traffic later that month at Shrewsbury shed. No.73125 was already at Shrewsbury whilst 73127-73134 would follow over the next three months. The Western Region did not really take to the Caprotti's and within two years 73125-73134 had been transferred to Patricroft where they were accepted and worked from there until the end of steam at that depot.

Derby works had always been associated with the 'Jinty' 0-6-0T so it was no surprise to find two of them, 47612 of Northampton shed, and 47604 of Workington, in the works yard on 8th July 1956, having had a full repaint after general overhaul. Both engines are from a batch built in 1928 by Beardmore. No.47604 was amongst the seventy-three 0-6-0T's withdrawn in 1962 and was cut up at BR works. No.47612 lasted a little while longer, until December 1966 in fact and was amongst the last of the class. It ended up in a private scrapyard in Shettleston.

The pioneer LMS main line 1,600 h.p. diesel electric locomotive No.10000 was built at Derby works and released to the Operating Department during the last month of LMS control. Sister engine 10001, also Derby built, was not put into traffic until July 1948 but from thereon both engines worked from Camden depot, usually together, hauling the premier WCML passenger express trains until the introduction of the English Electric Type 4's in the late 1950's. The 16-cylinder engines used by these locomotives were supplied by English Electric and much valuable data was gained during the trial period undertaken by these twins. Derby works had the responsibility for maintaining the pair, along with numerous other odds and ends, and on the 8th July 1956 No.10000 was in the Erecting shop with a few bumps and scratches to its paintwork besides sporting a new panel on the transition curve of its front body. Neither locomotive was considered for preservation despite their pedigree and the influence they must have had on BR's main line diesel policy. 10000 had the distinction, if such is possible, of being cut up where so many LMS 'Coronation' Pacifics had ended their days - Cashmores yard at Great Bridge, in January 1968. No.10001 went for scrap in a less distinguished yard - Cox & Danks, Acton.

(opposite) BR's first attempt at producing main line diesel locomotives began in November 1950 when Ashford works pushed out the first of three box fronted and long bogie diesel electrics. Numbered 10201, the prototype was sent to Stewarts Lane for trials on the Southern Region. Nine months later 10202 emerged from the same workshop but went to the London Midland Region at Derby for a short period to do trials on the main line out of St Pancras after which it returned to the Southern at Nine Elms. Both locomotives were rated at 1760 h.p. and clocked up considerable mileage during the next few years. In March 1954 the third and final member of the trio, 10203 rated at 2000 h.p., was put into traffic from Brighton works. It too was allocated to the SR at first and also worked from Nine Elms on the South Western section. Maintenance for these large main line diesels was entrusted to Derby, where experience with diesel motive power was in abundance even at this early stage of the BR diesel age. All three locomotives eventually moved permanently to the London Midland Region in 1955, working on the WCML. On 8th July 1956, No.10201 was receiving treatment to its prime mover and generator at Derby works, or at least it had been on the previous day. Work would resume again on Monday to get it back into traffic. Originally all three of the 1Co-Co1's had black livery with a silver-grey waistband but on moving to the LMR they were painted green with black and orange lining. Eventually, after 'doings the rounds' on the Region, all three ended up at Willesden. With the coming of the English Electric Type 4's in the late 1950's, these non-standard diesel electrics, which had a BR LMR power rating of 5MT began the slow rundown to redundancy and, after periods 'in store' at Derby, they were condemned during December 1963. However, they were then stored for four years before they too ended up at Cashmores scrapyard in Great Bridge.

The former Midland Railway engine shed at Derby consisted two square 'roundhouses' with a third turntable and radiating roads outside forming another shed albeit without walls and roof. Three occupants around the external table on the 8th July 1956 included the pioneer 'Crab' No.42700, Johnson 2P No.40513, and Stanier Class 5 No.44851. Except for the final five months of its existence, the 'Crab' from Bury was to spend the whole of its forty-year working life in the Lancashire and Yorkshire area in what was basically the old LMS Central Division. What of the final five months - they were spent at Birkenhead in Cheshire which although only a mile or so across the Mersey from Lancashire, does not count. The 4-4-0 did not have long to wait for its final call into works whilst the Millhouses based Stanier had started its career at Derby in November 1944 and it was amongst the last of the BR steam being withdrawn in March 1968 by Newton Heath shed.

Besides the locomotive works at Derby, the town also had a large Carriage and Wagon works where on Saturday 14th April 1956 some interesting passenger vehicles, current and former, awaited the photographer. The following three illustrations show a few of the gems on view. The first carriage is part of an ex Maryport & Carlisle 'narrow' set in new BR lined red livery. The legend on the end panel reads:- M&C NARROW SET *Return to Whitehaven*.

This 1909 built Midland clerestory brake was in the hands of the Engineers Department, its fine lining having long gone, covered by layers of black paint. But, it still looks nice and has an certain air of elegance about it.

Another Midland clerestory brake but from 1908. It appeared to still be in passenger service but if it ever saw its fiftieth birthday I will never know.

LMS Class 3 'Atlantic' tank No.41947 at Toton shed in September 1956. One of a batch of ten built at Derby in 1927 for working the London, Tilbury, Southend lines, this engine emerged with the LMS number 2129 which it carried for over twenty years until BR renumbered it along with the rest of the thirty-five strong class. On the LTS the class were allocated to Plaistow, Shoeburyness and Tilbury but as electrification ousted them from the passenger services, they took employment anywhere that would have them. Basically they ended at former Midland Division depots such as Toton. Withdrawal started in 1951 but it took ten years before the class was finally dealt with and 41947 was the last, being condemned in November 1960. Although Crewe, Derby and Stratford took a hand in their demise, the class became early candidates for the private scrapyards.

BR 9F No.92050 at Toton, 9th September 1956. This engine had arrived here new exactly twelve months previously from Crewe and was the first of many Standard 9F's to arrive at the shed. Already wearing a thick coat of grime, the engine had probably never been cleaned since arrival. During that year it had gone on loan to Kingmoor in the November for a few weeks but returned to join the growing contingent of 9F's congregating at 18A.

Trent was one of the most important junctions on the Midland Railway network with trains from the Erewash valley line finding routes to the west, south-west, south and east. The line from Derby found routes to the south, east and north whilst the line from Nottingham had the choice of south, south-west, west or north. Of course then there was the route from Leicester which could choose south-west, west, north, or east. It appeared complicated and could well have been dubbed the 'Spaghetti Junction' of its time but the trains were chaperoned through by a competent band of signalmen who knew the place inside out and needed seven signalboxes to do the job. On 24th December 1955, 'Jubilee' No.45560 PRINCE EDWARD ISLAND runs through towards the Trent bridge with an express from Nottingham to St Pancras via Leicester.

On a glorious day during the early months of 1957 rebuilt Johnson 3F 0-6-0 No.43251 makes its way toward Toton yard past the Trent Station North signal box with a train of coal empties.

Class D16/3 No.62571 calls at Trent station with a Derby (Midland) to Lincoln train in March 1957. The 'Clauds' were newcomers to this service which ran over the former Midland line via Nottingham and Newark. Five of the former Great Eastern 4-4-0's were transferred to Lincoln shed in early 1957 to take the place of the D11 'Directors' which previously worked the services. Their appearance at Trent certainly made a nice change from the endless ex MR and LMS locomotives threading the rails here. No.62571 was chosen by the East Midlands branch of the Railway Correspondence & Travel Society to head their annual railtour, *EAST MIDLANDER No.9*, in 1957 to York and back. With the continuous delivery of diesel multiple units for cross country and medium distance services in 1958, the 'Clauds' reign on the Derby-Lincoln trains was short and by January 1959 the last example allocated at Lincoln - 62571 - was withdrawn. What of Trent station itself ? The inevitable closure, because of the dwindling number of passengers, came on New Years Day 1968.